The ancestor of all ZÜNDAPP opposed-piston models was the 1932 K 400.

A Legend on Wheels ZÜNDAPP KS 601 the "Green Elephant"

by Reiner Scharfenberg

When Fritz Neumeyer, already a successful industrialist in other areas, visited the Berlin Automobile and Motorcycle Show in 1921, he made the decision to start manufacturing motorcycles in Nuremberg. No one could have believed that this enterprise, after just a few years, would hold a leading position among the producers of motorized two-wheelers.

With the idea of producing "the motorcycle for everybody," Neymeyer had shown an entrepreneur's long-range view: filling a hole in the market and using the experience gained in his other large-scale production of dependable goods to offer reliable high quality that rose above the products of the countless little workshops of the time.

After the upswing in competition of the postwar years, 28,047 motorcycles left the Zündapp manufacturing plants in 1929 alone. In the world economic crisis, production fell abruptly to 10,639 units in 1930 and only 1,790 in 1931.

Zündapp sought to oppose the downward trend with a completely new motorcycle program. Under the leadership of designers Richard and Xaver Küchen, there arose by the end of 1932 a varied new array of models that were displayed at the Berlin Auto Show in 1933.

Along with the Derby models, with 175 cc one-cylinder two-stroke block-construction motors with toothed gears, dependable chain drive, and tubular frame, the K models appeared with a series of new design features. They stood out from the broad spectrum of competitors' vehicles with the following design features:

- Multicylinder four-stroke motors in block construction, of their own design and manufacture;
- Good-looking pressed-steel frames;
- Elastic cardan drive via chain drive;
- Four-speed ball shifting as in automobiles;
- Extensive covering of all drive-train parts.

Keeping in mind the success of BMW's opposed-piston models with various consumers and in the sporting realm, Zündapp production included the following model types:

- K 200 with two-stroke one-cylinder block motor;
- K 400 with four-stroke two-cylinder (boxer = opposed piston) block motor;
- K 500 with four-stroke two-cylinder (boxer) motor;
- K 600 with four-stroke four-cylinder (double boxer) block motor;
- K 800 with four-stroke four-cylinder (double boxer) block motor.

Despite the technical superiority of this model program over the numerous competitors, Zündapp could scarcely have survived in a long-term economic crisis. When the National Socialists seized power, business began to boom again. Broad strata of the population were receiving incomes again. Tax decreases for the purchase of cars and motorcycles allowed sales by ve-

Only 25 of the first four-cylinder Zündapp 600 cc model were built, to be replaced as early as 1934 by the K 800.

hicle manufacturers to rise markedly already in 1933. At the beginning of September, Zündapp finished its 100,000th motorcycle since the firm's origin—a K 500.

This look backward into the Zündapp firm's history within the framework of its KS 601 model's history has a reason; with the creation of the opposed-piston "boxer" model, the ancestor of the "Green Elephant" came into being.

The Ancestry

The prototype of the K 400, the smallest boxer model, was finished in 1932. In the following year, 212 of them rolled off the assembly lines and were offered at a price of 1,195 Reichsmarks.

The 1- hp engine, on account of its carburetor type (with air filter), had long air intakes through the engine housing, and the cylinder to the vertical valves in the cylinder head. The powerplant ran quietly, which was typical of this cylinder arrangement. Other attributes, such as plug axles or turning handgrips, stressed the modern technical concept.

Production of the K 400 was soon halted in favor of the K 500, for 1,504 units

of this more powerful, 12.5 hp version in parallel production had already been sold in 1933, at a price only 55 Reichsmark above that of the K 400.

Another large-volume model, the S 500, with an 18 hp, four-stroke, one-cylinder two-valve motor and double-tube frame—the Zündapp motorcycle that sold best in 1931—was still offered in 1933 at the same price as the K 500, but in 1932 not a single motorcycle of this type had been built.

The four-cylinder K 600 and K 800 models were externally very similar. These bottom-controlled motors also had just one carburetor. The K 600 motor produced 15 hp at 4300 rpm, the K 800 motor 20 hp, likewise, at 4300 rpm.

Since only 25 of the K 600 had been sold in 1933, production ended that same year, for in 1933 185 of the flagship K 800 had been sold, and in 1934, still at a price of 1,550 Reichsmarks, 662 of them had been sold.

The silky-soft running of the four-cylinder engine had won renown, as had its outstanding suitability for sidecar use. These qualities naturally encouraged the Wehrmacht, being equipped under the new

regime, to order large numbers of the K 500 and K 800 as special Wehrmacht models.

BMW also produced boxer models—such as the R 32—with bottom-controlled motors, but since 1928 had also built top-controlled motors for the R 47. These motors were more powerful, and with these motorcycles BMW scored countless sporting victories that made for effective advertising.

Thus, it was just a matter of time before Zündapp, with its wealth of good ideas and its products that gained popularity with their elegant looks and quiet-running motors, produced a sporting version.

In 1935 the prototype of a long series of successful KS models, the KS 500, appeared. The designation stood for "Kardan Sport 500."

Still using the engine block of the K 500, aluminum cylinder heads were added to the cast cylinders, with rocker arms activating new dropped valves beneath the individual valve covers now typical of all KS models.

Every cylinder had a flanged Amal carburetor. The intake air came from a cen-

4

tral air filter. The shock-absorber mounts were cast into the cylinders.

Under the motor was a large ribbed oilpan, and a foot-pedal automat was added to the basic gearbox of the K models. The short-stroke motor (69 mm bore, 66.6 mm stroke) produced 24 hp at 5200 rpm.

This performance satisfied even the most pampered sporting drivers, but so much power in a solo motorcycle went far beyond the technical limits of the optically handsome but not very flex-free pressed-steel frame, no matter how much one tried to improve the roadholding with braces and oleopneu-matic forks.

For solo use, the KKS had been developed parallel to the KS 500 in 1937, its designation standing for "Kardan-small frame Sport 500."

In 1938 the displacement was enlarged to 600 cc, with 75 mm bore and 67.6 mm stroke. This increased the power to 28 hp at 4700 rpm. In contrast to the KS 500 models, the kS 600 had only one Amal carburetor with a diameter of 25.4 mm. The gears could be changed with combined hand and foot shifting. Series production began in February 1938.

Civilian production was limited as of March 2, 1939, because of type limitation regulations on motor vehicle production. Officially, this so-called Schell Plan was supposed to result in more practical production methods, lower prices, and simpler spare-parts supply, but it was really part of the preparation for war. The last delivery to a civilian customer took place on March 15, 1940.

From 1938 to 1941, 18,000 of the KS 600 were built—naturally, most of them were for the Wehrmacht.

KS 750

Originally, the kS models and the K 800 were meant to be fast road-sport machines not built for wartime use, and certainly not for sidecar use in rough country. During military testing and use it was seen that such vehicles did not always stand up to rough wartime action and higher demands.

In Berlin in 1937, Hans-Friedrich Neumeyer (son of the firm's founder, who died in 1935) had suggested a very heavy motorcycle with integrated sidecar—still based on the KS 600 concept—but it soon was seen that something new was needed for military purposes.

With these different—military—standpoints in mind, urgent developmental work on a motorcycle with integrated sidecar, and with the sidecar wheel also driven, began. In 1938-39 a first dummy with a 700 cc motor was built on the KS basis, without retaining previous design details in a simply strengthened version. Its use as a solo cycle was, on principle, not intended.

A 750 cc motor with valves activated from above was decided on, and its cylinders were mounted at five degrees above the horizontal. Unlike the usual chain drive of the Zündapp boxer models, the motor was integrated with a four-speed gearbox that included a reverse gear. Shifting was done by two hand levers to the right, at tank level. Rear-wheel drive included a cardan shaft and geared differential.

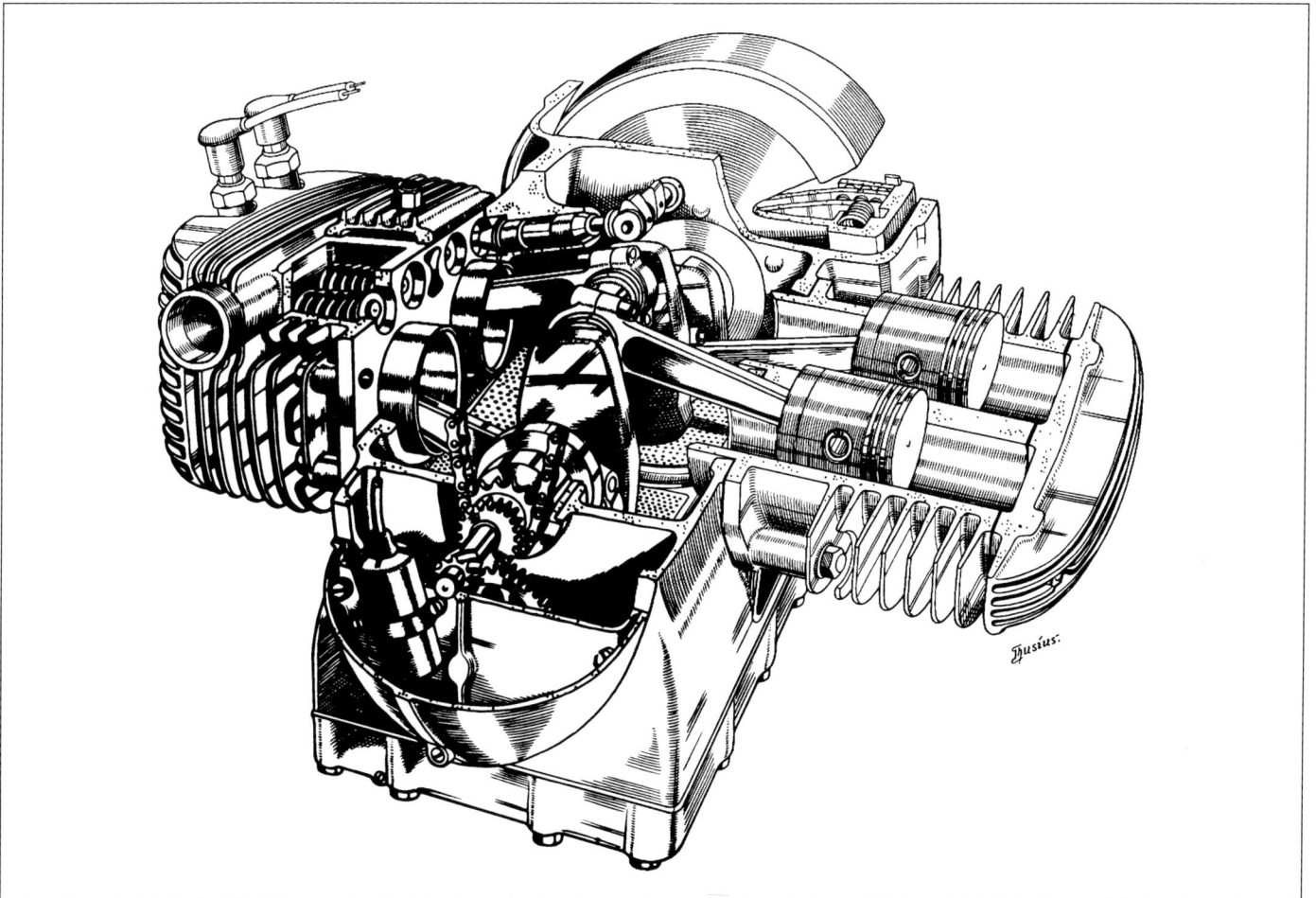

Thusius cutaway drawing of the four-cylinder 600 or 800 cc motor.

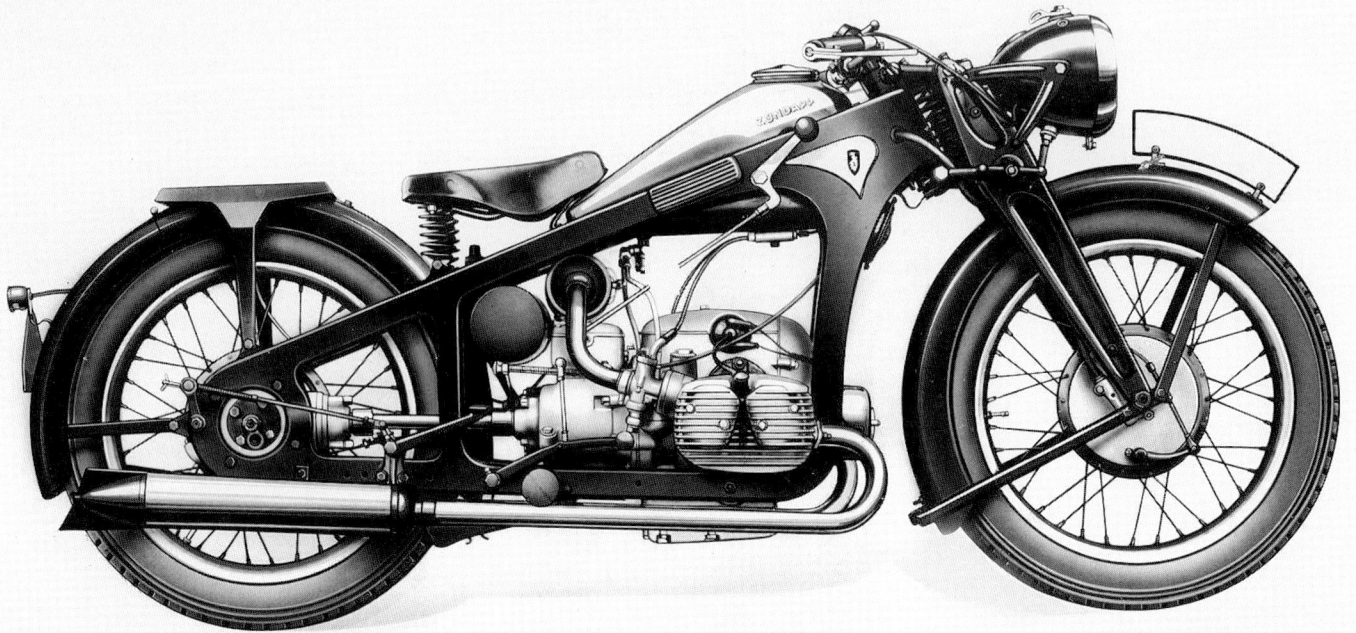

The first machine with overhead valve control was the KS 500m, which came on the market in 1936.

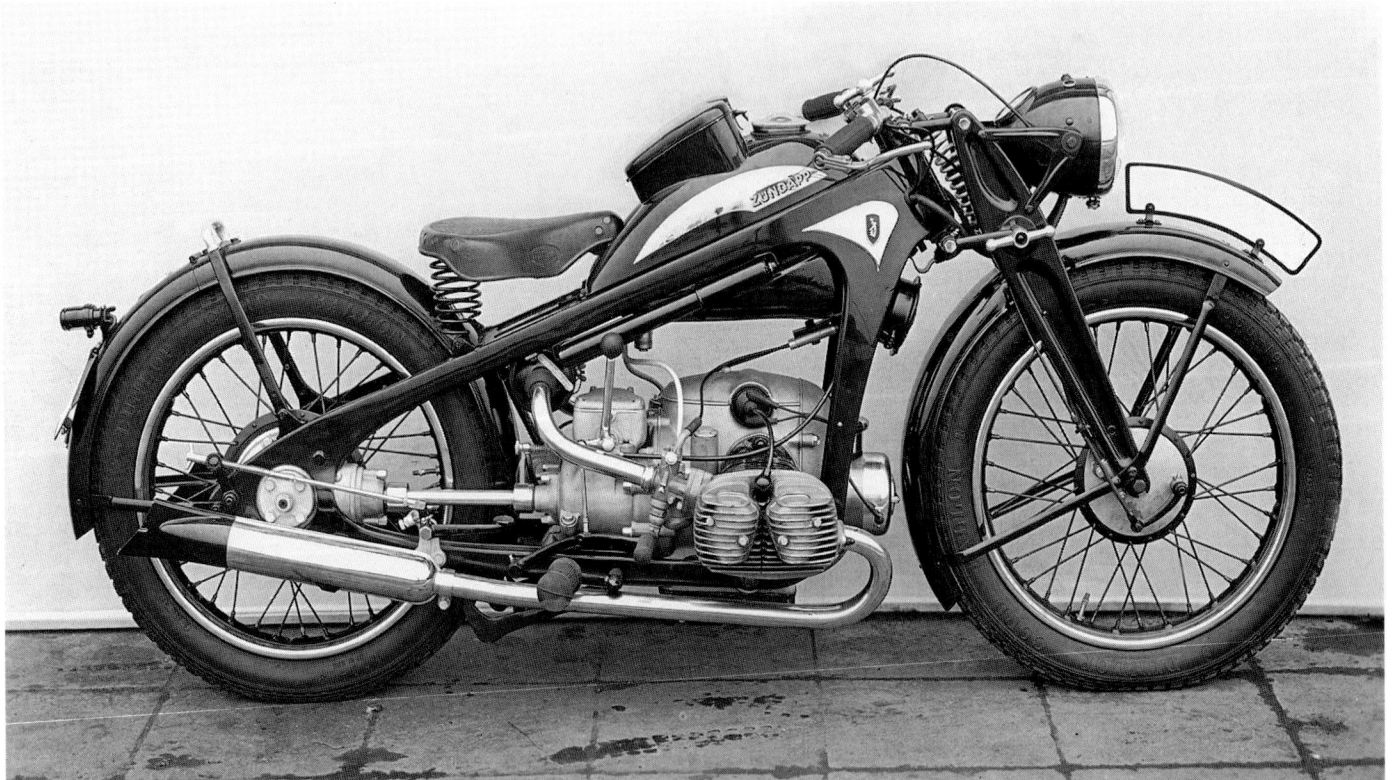

The sporting variation of the KS 500 had a lighter pressed-steel frame and was called KKS 500.

The KS 600 was originated in 1937 as a sidecar cycle, and especially for official use.

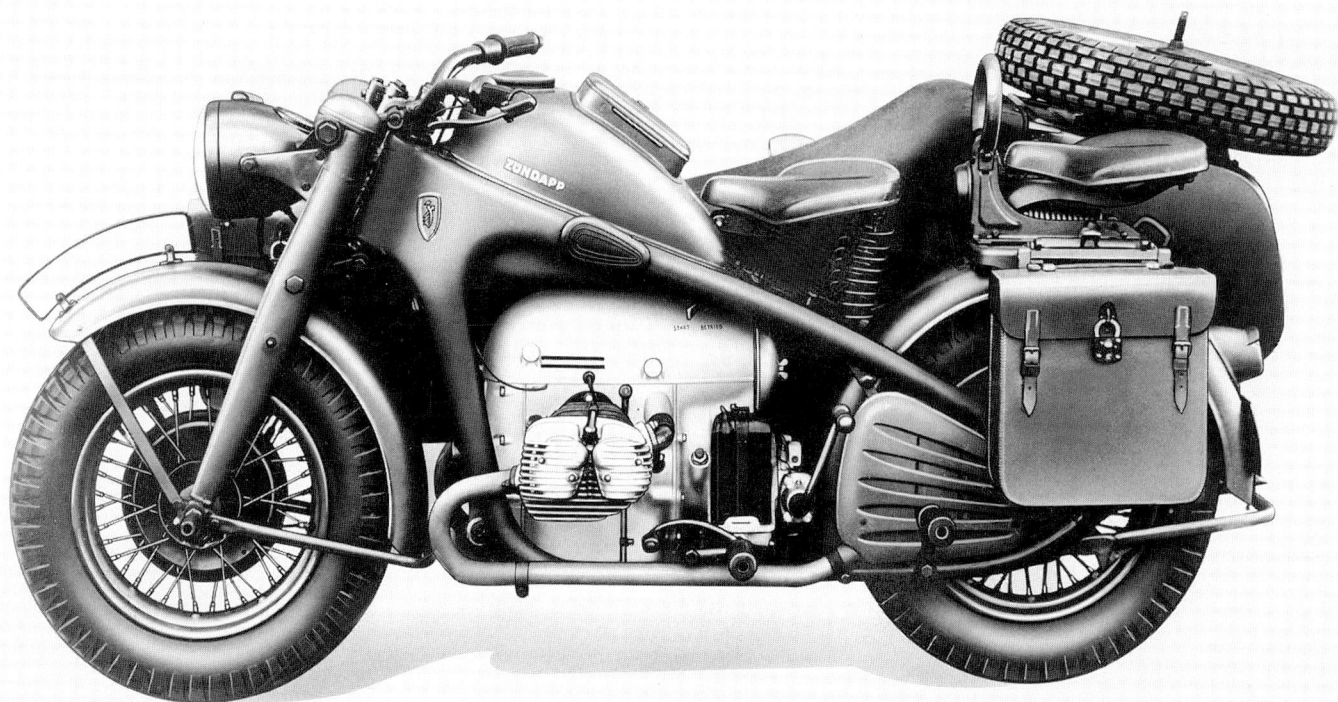

The very heavy KS 750 cycle was developed especially for use in World War II.

A sidecar motorcycle in tow on the eastern front during World War II.

Unlike all the Zündapp cardan motorcycles (including the postwar KS 601) with chain drive, the KS 750 had a gearbox with reverse gear and off-road gears. A specialty was the power equalization system with locking differential in the rear axle drive, whereby 60% of the power was to the rear wheel and 40% to the driven sidecar wheel.

With a further shifting system to the rear-wheel drive, the differential could be locked. This special Zündapp development allowed a divided power flow, with 60% going to the rear wheel and 40% to the sidecar wheel. The tires, of 4.50 x 16 size, were like those of the contemporary Volkswagen. With these big oleopeumatically braked wheels, the machine had remarkable ground clearance.

At the same time, BMW had developed such a rig, but without the important divider differential, without oleopneumatic brakes, and with a side-valve motor. In comparisons, the superiority of the Nuremberg machine was obvious, and the Army Weapons Office suggested that BMW copy it, which the Munich firm refused to do. Under massive pressure "from above," an approximation of the most important components was agreed on, whereby Zündapp had to do without any licensing agreement. Thus, the Wehrmacht obtained two very similar "over-heavy" motorcycles.

Series production of the KS 750 began in 1941 when 288 were built. In 1942 a KS 750 was the 250,000th motorcycle to leave the factory, and by war's end the Wehrmacht had ordered 18,236 of them. From 1942 on, the KS 750 was the only

motorcycle type that Zündapp built. Within the parameters of all-out munitions production, parts of the factory produced ammunition, starter motors for aircraft under license from Bosch, and some 10,000 electric aggregates with the stationary KS 600 powerplant. By 1945, Zündapp also built the explosive tank designed by Borgward. 3,600 of these were built, each with a Steib armored hull and a simple two-cylinder two-stroke cast iron motor.

The Zündapp factory was badly damaged in the air raids and final battles around Nuremberg. Plundering took what little remained.

In May 1945, some 150 former workers began to remove rubble, but there was no way to resume motorcycle production. The Allied control council had envisioned a yearly production of 10,000 cycles with a maximum of 60 cc engines in all four occupation zones. Zündapp kept its head over water by producing urgently needed milling magazines and other objects for everyday use. In 1946 the dismantling of the factory was even threatened as a reparation payment, but intensive negotiations with German and American officials resulted in this cruel fate being avoided.

By 1948, KS 750 rigs were still assembled out of spare parts, with 464 cycles

delivered to the Allies. In 1948-49 a civilian version—especially for export—was even considered. Zündapp was able to resume motorcycle production in a modest way as early as 1947, turning out the almost unchanged prewar DB 200 model. But in 1949 and 1950 the last 381 KS 600 cycles were also built, after the displacement limit had been abolished by the Allied officials. Most of the cycles, fitted with Steib official-type sidecars, were used by the police and the border patrol.

KS 601—The Green Elephant
Zündapp production was fully spoken for by the demand for the 200 Derby models, and at first there was no intention of modernizing the twelve-year-old KS 600 sidecar rig that had been taken back into the program, now that the displacement limit had been abolished.

In 1948-49 work had begun on various test models of a KS 250. A flat four-stroke block motor with cardan drive had been installed in a double-tube frame with telescopic fork and direct rear wheel suspension. In terms of its design, the motorcycle—including its motor—looked very similar to the contemporary British motorcycles. This KS 250, though, never went into production.

Unlike all the other Zündapp boxers, the KS 750 had its cylinders mounted at 5-degree angles above the horizontal for the sake of better ground clearance.

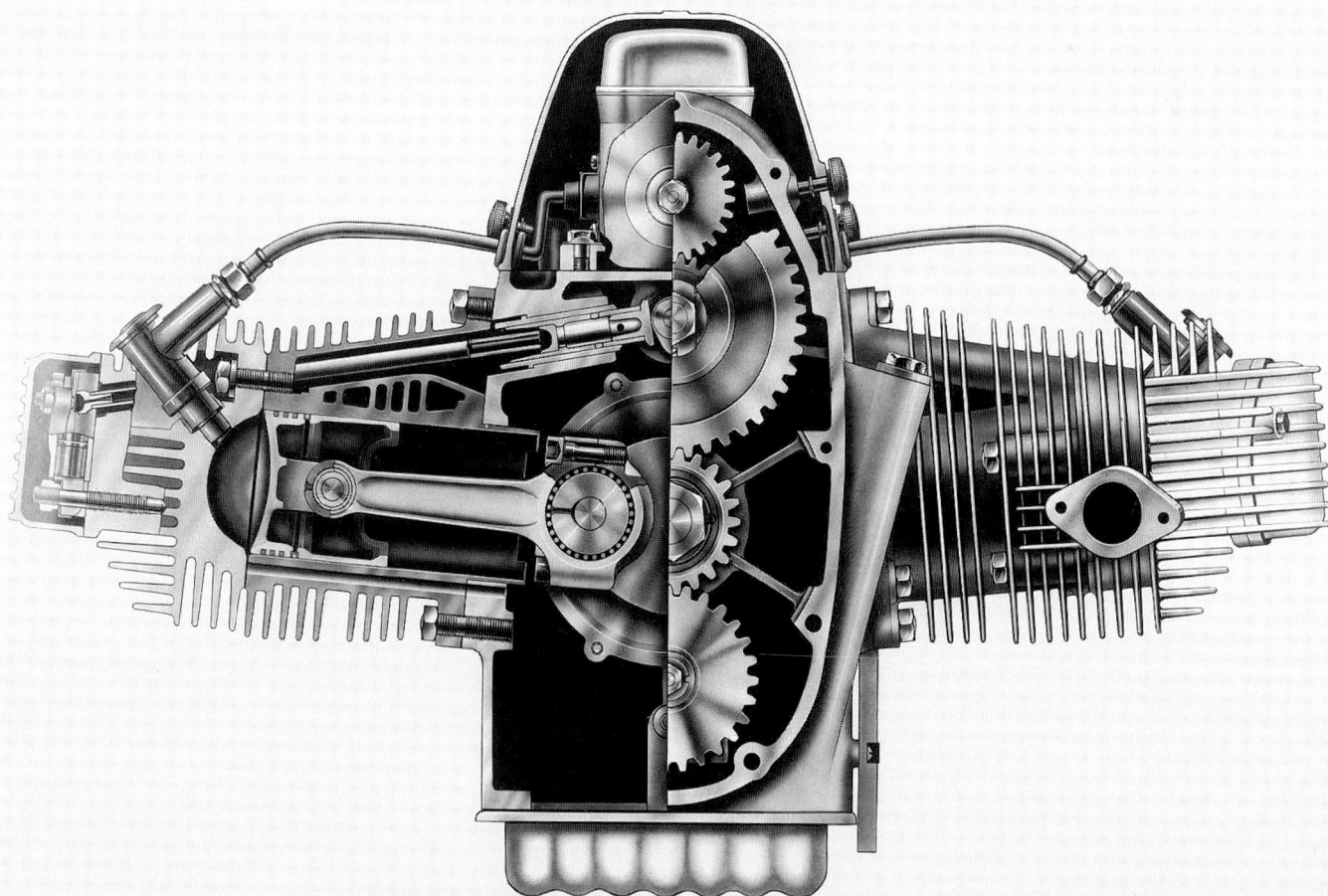

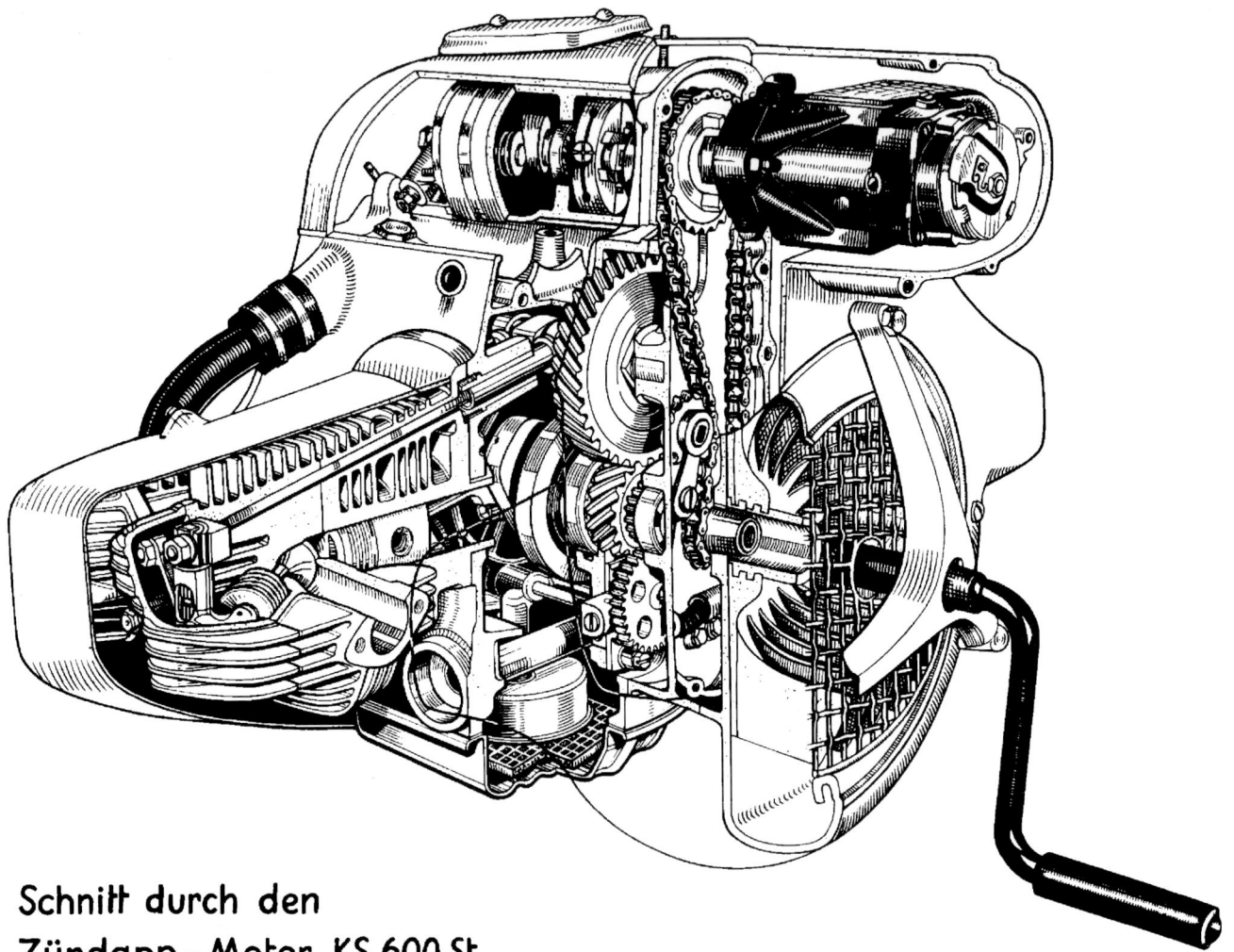

Schnitt durch den Zündapp – Motor KS 600 St

During the war the 600 cc motorcycle engine was combined with this air-cooled aggregate unit for various testing purposes.

But a member of the design bureau put big things into motion with a joke. He retouched a photo of the KS 250 by adding the motor of the KS 600 to it.

Chief designer Ernst Schmidt, who was already involved with Zündapp boxers since the thirties and had returned to Nürnberg after working on the NSU track cycle during the war, liked this picture. A KS 600 motor, with different cylinder heads and sheet-metal vent covers, was mounted in a KS 250 frame.

Director Neumeyer and his brother-in-law, Dr. Eitel-Friedrich Mann, who had entered the firm as business manager in 1946, were also interested in this project, and gave permission for developmental work on a motorcycle that naturally needed a stronger frame, a more stable telescopic fork, and larger brakes than the KS-250 experiment.

This work came along just at the right time. Zündapp had always built more motorcycles than BMW, but had never been able to equal the image of the Munich firm.

Now an opportunity was seen to build a better motorcycle than the BMW R 51/2, which had come on the market in October 1949 and had since been revised.

It took until October 1949 before the first prototype had been prepared by Zündapp.

The Chassis
The double-member frame—like that of the BMW—had two strong bottom members. But instead of their central tube under the tank, two frame tubes ran through from the steering head to the rear-wheel springs. Likewise, instead of having one vertical strut in front of the rear wheel, a strong welded-in panel, on which the spring of the swing saddle was supported, ran from the rear fender to below the tank. The lower frame members were also welded on with reinforcing panels in front of the rear fender and under the gearbox. The steering head also had a sturdy brace to the upper and lower frame members. Welded-on sidecar attachment bolts were included for

the sake of sidecar utility and rough off-road use.

In the first test models, the rear axle was still mounted ahead of the rear-wheel suspension, which consisted of one spring each above and below the axle mount. In the guiding tube of the suspension was an additional spring, with an attachment in addition to the rubber buffers. At 64 mm, the suspension had more total play than did comparable products. During the course of development, the axle was moved in back of the rear-wheel suspension.

The spring play in the front fork was almost twice as long. The immersion tubes and fork bridges consisted of forged aluminum. The forward axle was held by a two-piece cramp-iron, which was held by the set-screw in the immersion tube and allowed for quick dismantling. In the long boxes of the immersion tubes the hard-chromed standing tubes moved. The smaller, softer springs originally contacted the two coil springs in each tine of the fork, with the larger springs following under greater pressure.

The KS 600 was produced in a slightly modified version from 1949 on.

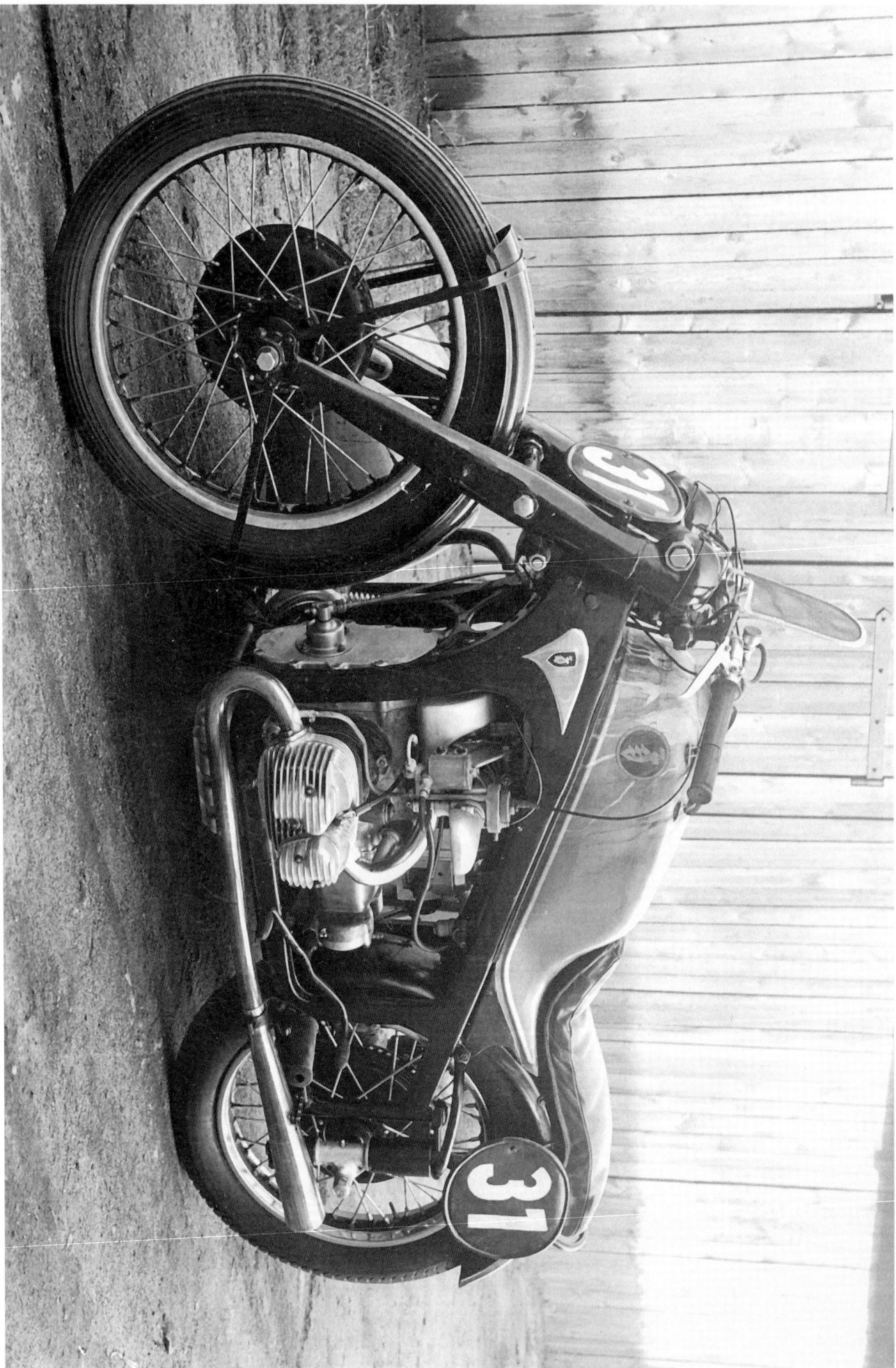

With this 600 cc supercharged sidecar racing machine, developed with little works support by Oskar Pillenstein of Fuerth, Loni Neussner and Fred Minderlein of Nuremberg became Germany's best private drivers of 1949.

Into the photo of a KS 250, which never went into production, a design team member inserted the motor of the KS 600. That gave the fortunate impetus for the development of the KS 601.

After slightly modifying the KS 250 frame, a KS 600 motor was installed, making the photo study a reality.

The first prototype of the KS 601—still painted black...

...and seen here with different tank decorations.

With this brochure, which still shows the prototype, advertising of the KS 601 began. This version of the motorcycle, though, never went into series production.

The fork horns, in fact, gained an oil filler, but that only lubricated the sliding boxes. The fork suspension was produced by a separate shock absorber, with its attachment projecting out over the fork bridge between the fork spars. The shock absorber originally was attached to a transverse yoke, but in the production model screws were used on the holding bow of the fender. With the axle through the steering-head tube, pulling on the star grip on the upper fork bridge over friction panels could make the fork contact harder to move, so as to decrease swinging in the sidecar movement. The runback of the front wheel was 71 mm at a steering angle of some 64 degrees.

On the rims of the spoked wheels, size 2.15 B x 19, size 3.50-19 tires were mounted for solo use. For sidecar use, a rear tire of 4.00-19 size was used.

The Brakes

At first the wheels had full-hub brakes made of steel, with 230 mm diameter and 25 mm active width. Later aluminum brakes, at first with the same measurements, were used, before the drums were made with cooling ribs.

The Motor

In the first prototype, an unchanged KS 600 motor was used, which required rebuilding the drive train on account of the rear-wheel suspension. The cardan shaft was

made with cross joints at both ends to equalize the spring movements. The gearbox was also rebuilt, with a makeshift solution sufficing for the prototypes. For series production, a newly designed gearbox top was needed, for in the previous carburetor chamber the big damp-air filter for the two-carburetor version was housed. The first motor with two 25 mm Bing carburetors could be installed in the second test vehicle in February 1950. The two openings right and left on the gearbox top, in which the intake pipes were mounted on the KS 600, were closed by caps.

The bore/stroke ratio remained unchanged, with a bore of 75 mm and stroke of 67.6 mm (displacement 597 cc). With the compression at 1:6.4 to 1:6.7, the offi-

17

The pre-series model being tested at the Nürburgring. The designer of the KS 601, Ernst Schmidt, wears a peaked cap; with him are Georg Weiss (with goggles) and Gustav Keitel.

cial power was 28 hp at 4700 rpm, and the maximum torque was 4.56 mkg (or 45.6 Nm) at 4000 rpm. These were values that exceeded those of the contemporary Volkswagen.

The crankshaft was mounted in one ball bearing and two roller bearings. Unlike the pressed BMW crankshafts with undivided roller-bearing rod feet, the KS 601 motor had its piston rods attached to the one-piece crankshaft with divided feet. The crankshaft was introduced into the tunnel housing from the rear and inserted into the front roller bearing. Then, the rear roller bearing could be screwed on, along with the bearing cover and the crankcase. Then the needle cages were fitted with the needle bearings and set on the piston pivot. The bottom of the rod was done from the opposite side, and the rod was inserted from the other side. Finally, the rod screws could be put in and their nuts screwed on from the rod side.

The camshaft, mounted in roller bearings front and rear, was located in the middle of the housing above the crankshaft. The diagonally-toothed gear on the front

end of the crankshaft operated it. The material for the camshaft gear was one developed to lessen sound, a pressed fabric known as Novotex, the name meaning "new textile." Later, this combination of materials, already used in the automobile industry in the thirties, proved to be very sensitive. When the oil pressure in the suction bell of the oilpan decreased on account of increasing dirt in the big oil filter, it soon caused wear on the Novotex gear.

Ahead of the camshaft gear there was a second gear on the end of the crankshaft to operate the oil pump, which was mounted in the front wall of the housing. This simultaneously sent lubricating oil to the left rod bearing and the top of the housing. There, in the space of the KS 600 fuel injector, was an oil-warming chamber, from which the right rod bearing and the Novotex gear were supplied with oil under pressure. Oil was sprayed onto the camshaft and, via the pushrod tubes in the cylinders, outward to the needle-bearing rocker arms. The oil could run back into the oilpan through holes bored in the un-

dersides of the cylinders and cylinder heads.

In August 1953, the oil situation was changed extensively by the introduction of a modified engine block. This housing can be recognized by its lack of sprayers for the suction tubes of the KS 600. Because the divided filter that was used previously had been omitted during production of this motor, the closing cover of the filter chamber under the left cylinder, as well as the oil-warming chamber, had been eliminated. The oil under pressure was now conducted to the crankshaft, which was also modified, and to the camshaft.

A two-plate dry clutch in the swinging panel at the rear crankshaft bearing transmitted the engine's power to the gearbox. The swinging panel was likewise the clutch housing, and also included eight holes for the pressure springs. The clutch was operated mechanically by means of a cable.

The Gearbox
The gearbox mounted to the swinging-panel bell of the engine block contained

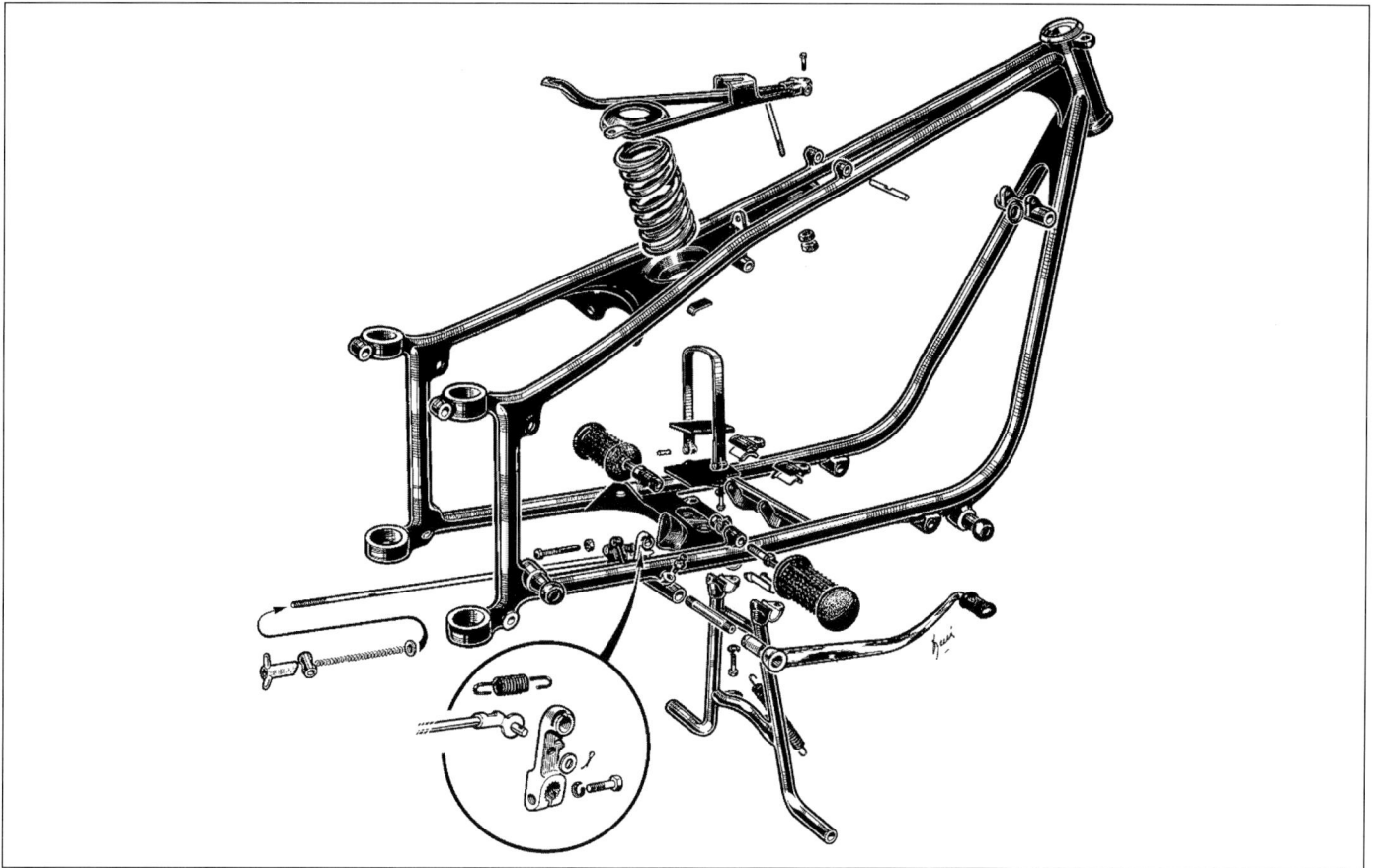

Frame of the KS 601.

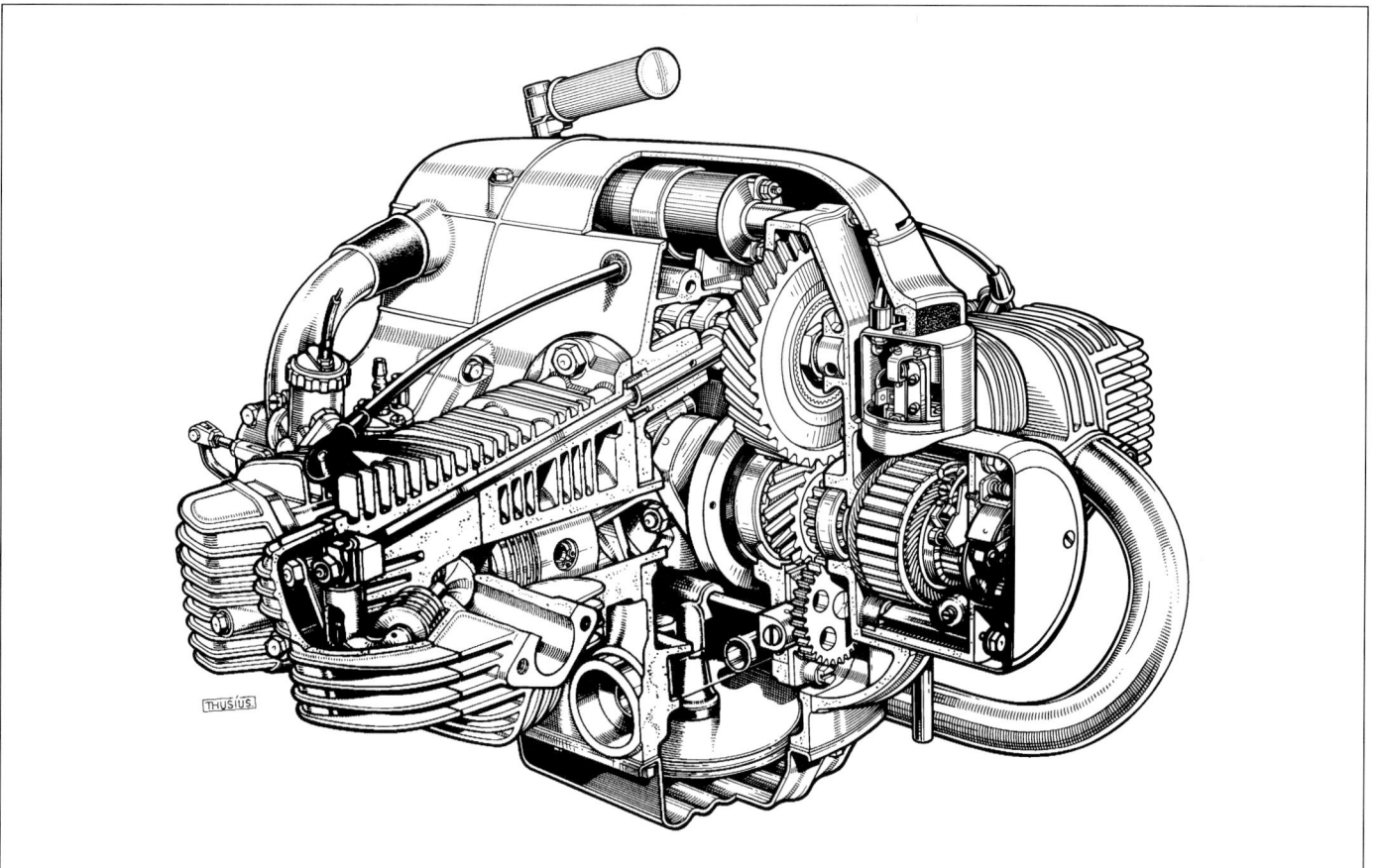

Motor of the KS 601.

The KS 601 motor and chain-drive gearbox.

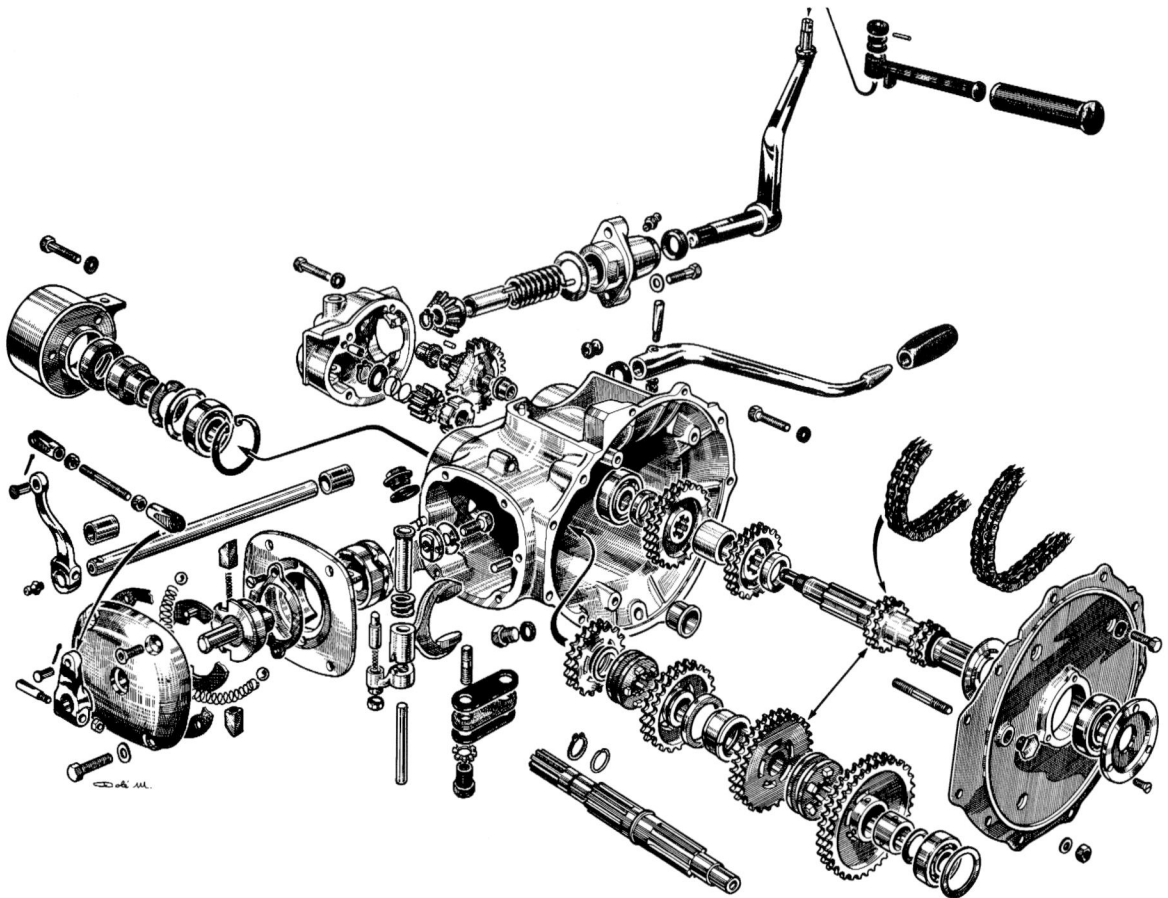

Exploded view of the gearbox with recognizable automatic shifting.

the usual Zündapp chain drive used since the introduction of the boxer models, with four speeds. The gears were linked by duplex chains, with gear changing done by a claw shift. In comparison with all other known designs, though, it was unusual.

When the foot shift pedal was activated, a shifting claw was set into pulling motion, drawing a transport hook far enough in the same direction to make the flap contact the stop panel of a guide panel. The necessary shifting movement was thus ended. An opposing flap was thus pushed backwards through the curving path of the guide panel into the shifting shaft and then came out of contact. Through a second hooking series the shifting element was automatically pulled back to the initial position via a rivet bolt—held by two steel balls in a pressure spring.

The transmission of the approximately 40 degrees of torque of the shifting cam into an axial movement took place as follows:

On the outer cover of the shifting cam a curved groove had been cut, through which the shifting path was turned into sideward motions. The exact points of the individual gears were controlled by deepenings into which a spring-mounted bolt moved in the various gears. The

Rear axle drive of the KS 601.

sideward movements of the fingers, which were guided by the curved course of the shifting cam, were converted into axial motion by the fixed shift lever via the carrying lever. Thereby the shifting forks were moved far enough on the driveshaft to move into the grooves for the appropriate gears. Thus, shifting was not done directly by the foot shift lever, but rather chosen more or less in advance, with the actual shifting done by spring pressure.

With the double chains, shocks coming from the rear wheel were dampened elastically, as the cardan drive with the two crosslinks and the multibelt shaft were regarded as too stiff for longitudinal equalizing.

The Electrics
The anchor of the 50-70 watt generator (Noris Plate Dynamo) was mounted directly on the ball joint mounted in roller bearings on the front of the casing. The ignition system (with its set of contact interruptors) stuck out of the housing from under a sheet-metal cover, as did the voltage regulator mounted on top of it. The double ignition coil was mounted lengthwise under a lid on top of the motor. The setting of the battery ignition (Noris DS 6/50/6) was done by hand.

A six-volt, 35-watt Bilux bulb in the headlight, with a 160 mm diameter, pro-

vided light at night. The tachometer and odometer, as well as the ignition lock, were located in the headlight casing.

The Paint
The first prototype—finished in October 1949—was painted black, and the sides of the tank were decorated differently: one side had double trim lines along the contours of the tank, while the other side had a set-off field around the Zündapp emblem.

But Director Neumeyer's favorite color was lime green. He decided that the second prototype, finished in February 1950, would have a black frame, but the tank, fenders, tool kit, fork cover, and light casings would be painted lime green; thus, the motorcycle differed from those of BMW, which were traditionally painted black.

Beginning with the second prototype, chromed flat oval exhaust pipes made by the Nürnberg firm of Leistritz replaced the first model's fishtail mufflers, and other details, like the fenders and the tool kit under the swinging saddle, were made to look better.

Testing
Naturally, the pre-series motorcycles were subjected to intensive tests. For long-term or final tests, they were taken in the autumn of 1950 to the Nürburgring, where

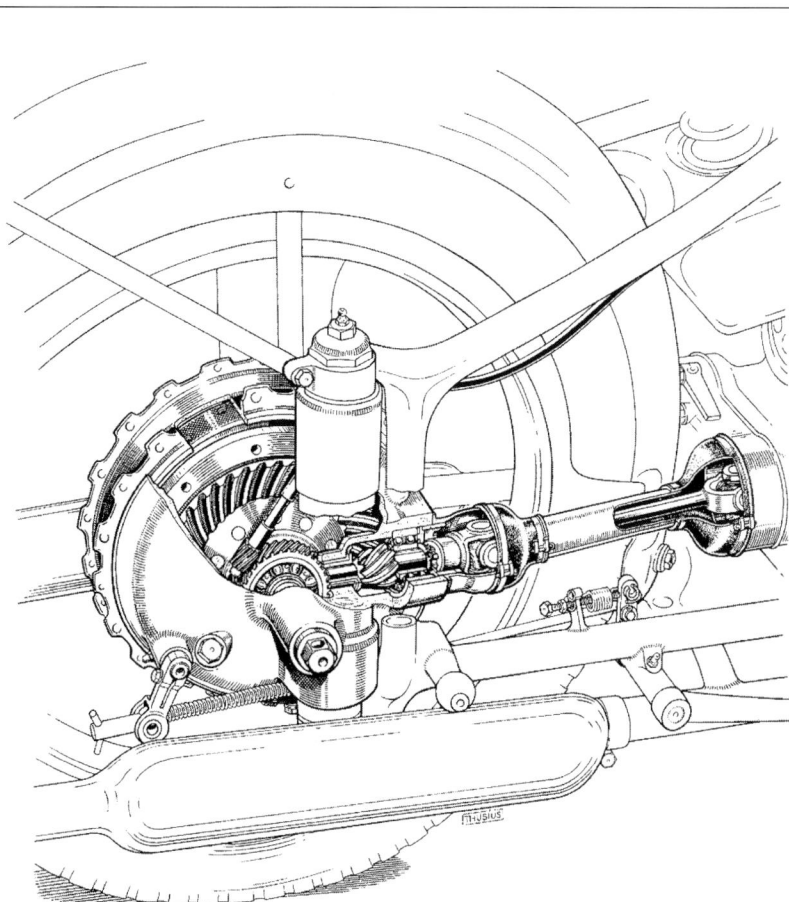

rability, but in the hands of its not so sporting owners it proved to be an extremely dependable motorcycle, with which one could drive the Autobahn solo at speeds over 150 kph, or up to 120 kph with a sidecar. The most noteworthy proof of its carrying ability was provided by the Langs, father-and-son travel reporters, who used a KS 601 rig for a 32,000-kilometer trip around the world. Watched by design chief Ernst Schmidt, the renowned cycle journalists Carl Hertweck, Helmut Hütten, and Helmut Werner Bönsch dismantled the motorcycle. They were very impressed by the meager signs of wear and the tremendous durability, for what the cycle had achieved under pressure far above that of normal use in the hands of non-specialists was a remarkable kind of material testing. To this day, this machine can be admired at the Two-wheel Museum in Neckarsulm. Although Zündapp made the most of this event for advertising, sales remained less than expected. In 1952, 1,650 cycles could be sold, this being 310 more than the BMW R 67, but in the same time period the Munich firm had sold 4,020 of the R 51/3, as well as 900 of the new top-class R 68. BMW's reputation gained the firm much export success, especially in the USA.

When Zündapp, looking especially to the U.S. market, brought out a KS 601 Sport model, BMW had already taken up the greatest share of the market.

In the KS 601 Sport, a modification of the pistons and camshaft had resulted in 34 hp at 6000 rpm. The clutch was fitted with twelve pressure springs instead of eight.

Externally, the Sport version was recognizable by the lack of a luggage rack, and by its chromed fuel tank. Despite having better driving qualities than the BMW (thanks to its expensively created wheel suspension), the KS 601 could not establish itself as a solo machine; it was branded as a sidecar cycle. The R 68, costing 725 DM more, was seen as the solo motorcycle—with sidecar potential.

Zündapp varied the colors to include ivory, black, and red, fitted the U.S. machines with a seat bench and high handlebars, and also met clients' wishes with extensive technical changes. In 1953, a version with a carburetor was produced for

solo and Royal sidecar cycles covered many a kilometer, and were also compared with, among others, a BMW R 51/2 and a Horax Regina.

Along with the test and race drivers Georg Weiss and Gustav Keitel, design chief Ernst Schmid devoted himself to his newest development, and the editor of "Das Motorrad," Karl Hertweck, who was known to be critical, expressed his views in No. 21 of 1950.

It was not until the summer of 1951 that the first production motorcycles could be delivered. Zündapp was not to blame for this delay. The problems arose from delivery delays of suppliers, who were pushed to the limits of their material and production capacities all over Germany by the ongoing German Economic Miracle.

The production lead of BMW was scarcely to be equaled. By that time BMW had been able to sell 5,000 of the R 51/2, a prewar design, and in 1951 the R 51/3 successor design—also with a 500 cc motor—came on the market. In answer to the new Zündapp, BMW also produced the 600 cc R 67. Although the R 67, at 2,875 Marks, was no less than 375 DM more expensive than the KS 601, the Munich firm was able to sell 1,645 of them. Zündapp, on the other hand, could only move 690 cycles, what with the delays.

In the specialist press, the new Zündapp produced enthusiasm in the form of positive test reports.

Since Carl Hertweck had entitled his big test in "Das Motorrad" (No. 25, 1951) "KS 601—The Green Elephant," the motorcycle had once and for all added this name to its factory designation. The name could scarcely have fit better, what with its weighty appearance and bullish power.

Not only in motor sports did the KS 601 earn an outstanding reputation for duthe Yugoslav Army, again using the engine block of the KS 600.

The sales of motorcycles of this caliber were clearly decreasing. After selling 1,113 in 1953, sales sank to 640 in 1954.

Officialdom, insurance firms, newspapers, and, not the least, the automobile industry succeeded in lobbying to give motorcycles and sidecars a negative image. A person who could not afford a car was no longer accepted, but was seen as a "rocker" with all the negative connotations, who was himself at fault if he exposed himself to wind and weather. Often enough, motorcyclists were denied admittance to taverns at that time. Yet their tax and insurance payments alone were almost twice as high as those for a car. Now, small cars were tremendously popular—though their technology was often questionable, and a VW Beetle, at less than 4,000 Marks, was less expensive than a Zündapp or BMW cycle and sidecar.

In 1955 Zündapp tried to do better on the American market with the KS 601 Elastik, featuring a swinging rear wheel. It was too late. Motorcycle firms with big names, such as NSU, Horex, or Triumph, ended their production. Goodly numbers

The rear wheel suspension.

of Bella-Rollers and S models still rolled off the Zündapp assembly lines. But the KS 601 numbers sank from 415 (1955) and 360 (1956) to 120 (1957) and 15 in 1958, the year in which the Nuremberg factory was sold to the Bosch firm. After moving into a Munich factory, the firm did not resume production of the KS 601, for the demand was too small. Only the spare parts department moved to Munich. In all, 5,003 of the KS 601 and KS 601 Sport had been built between 1950 and 1958.

The legend remained of the almost indestructible boxer motorcycle, which has maintained its groups of fans to this day.

"Green Elephants" Today

The numbers of "elephant drivers" very soon developed into a devoted community. The "elephant meeting" that continues to this day got its name in 1956, when KS 601 drivers first met at Solitude, near Stuttgart, on the first Saturday in January. Ernst Leverkus, chief tester for "Das Motorrad" and known in motorcycling circles as "Klacks," was a KS owner, and wanted to get together peacefully with other fans at a time when the general public preferred to stay home and keep warm. He could not have imagined what was to develop out of this meeting. Soon new lo-

cations for these meetings had to be found. At these meetings, or at the Salzburgring or the Nürburgring, the numbers of those who came with their motorcycles soon grew to the tens of thousands, though naturally the numbers of Zündapp KS 601 drivers were limited. In the winter of 1999, the 43rd annual meeting was held at Thurmansbang in the Bavarian Woods.

A comparatively large number of these cycles were spared the fate of many other motorcycles: a trip to the junkyard. Yet, keeping their KS cycles alive soon proved to be quite problematic for the owners, for after about five years, Zündapp, for financial reasons, sold the geeater part of their supply of spare parts to a Greek firm. For a long time, only a few used parts were available.

There had never been a factory service manual. "Das Motorrad" has done a great service with a richly illustrated, nine-section repair manual for the motor and gearbox (No. 24, 1959 to No. 6, 1960).

Used KS motorcycles could be bought fairly reasonably for a long time, for many motors were worn, especially in the area of their driveshaft and Novotex wheel, and regarded as irreparable for lack of replacement parts. Groups of owners were formed and helped each other, and since 1974 the

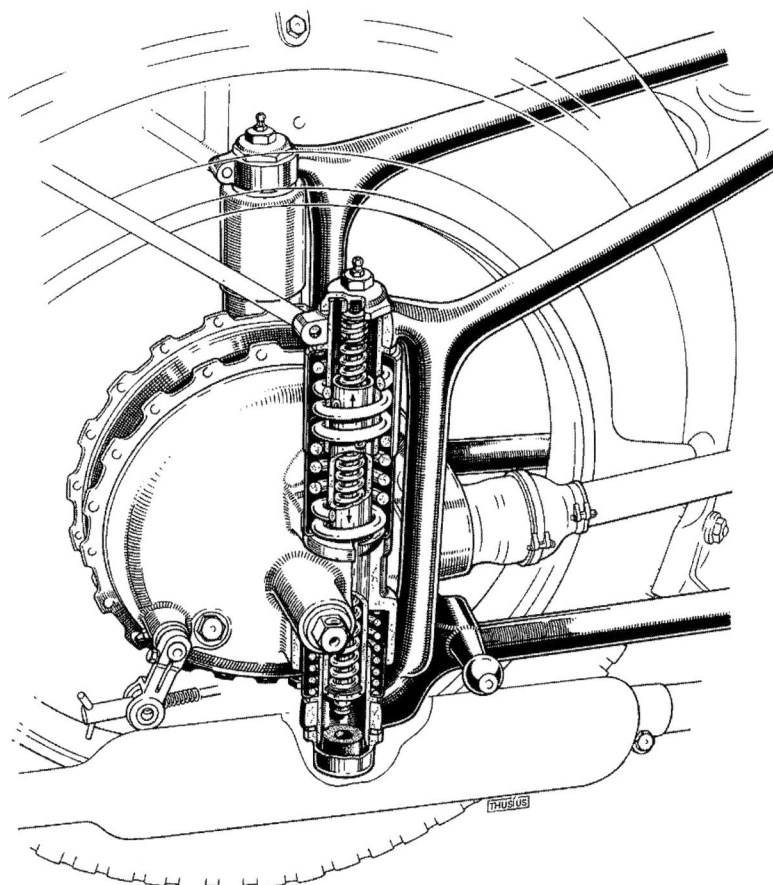

At the 1952 IFMA, Zündapp presented a cutaway model of the KS 601. This motorcycle is now at the Museum of Industry in Nürnberg.

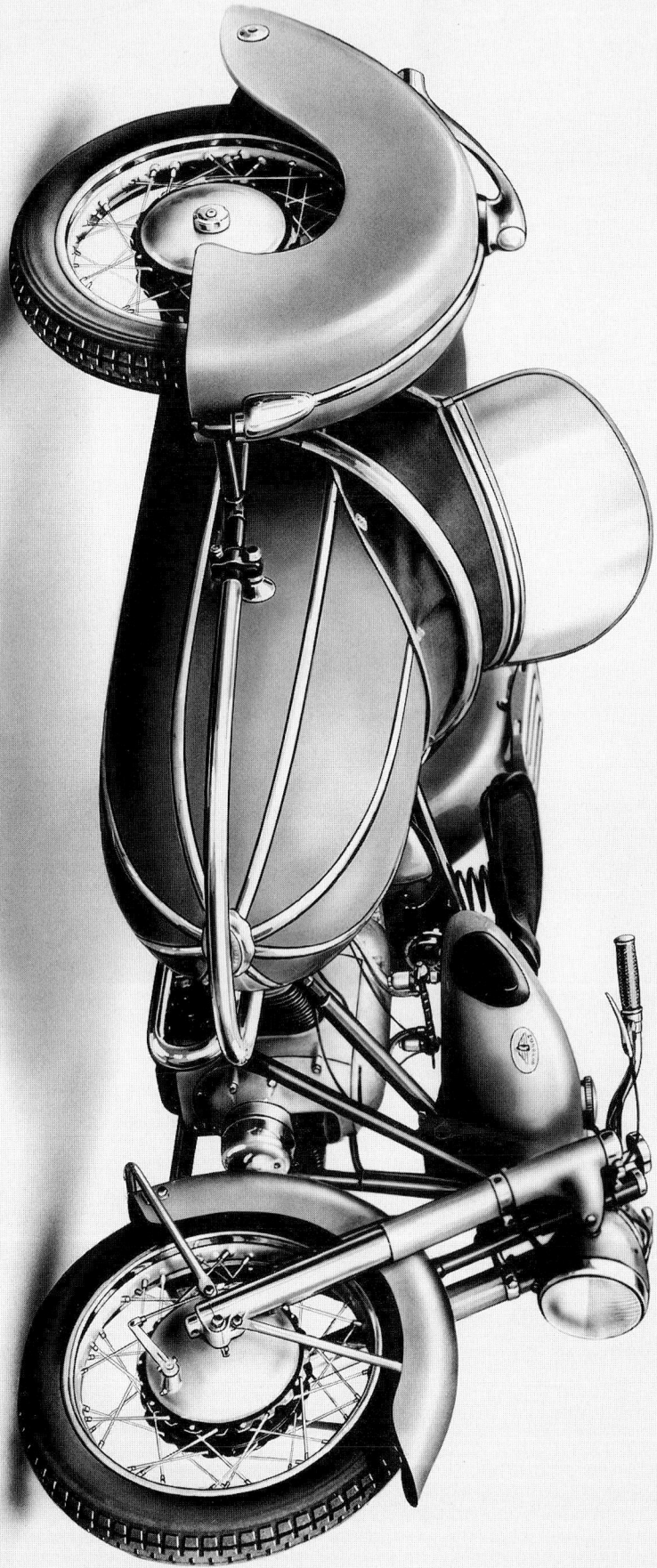

The KS 601 with official sidecar.

At the 1953 IFMA, Zündapp introduced its KS 601 Sport, recognizable by its aluminum hubs, lack of a luggage rack, and—on request—chromed fuel tank.

In 1956 bigger and quieter mufflers were introduced.

The KS 601 gained a rear-wheel swing, especially for the U.S. market, with the cardan shaft running into the right swinging tube.

A detailed view of the rear-wheel swing of the American KS 601.

The single-carburetor version for the Yugoslavian police.

Police cycles in the factory yard, ready for delivery.

Zündapp-KS 601-C e. V. club has existed, coordinating mutual assistance in obtaining spare parts for its barely 300 members. Some 120 members bought into a spare-parts fund at 200 DM apiece, the money being used in major efforts to obtain parts for members and keep the boxer motors alive. Only for this group are there new parts, which have to be paid for in full.

What is available ranges from replicas of original parts to modifications of other parts. For example, the crankshaft of the Citroen 2CV engine has been reworked to represent the dimensions of the old KS shaft after being dismantled at the shaft ends. New rod couplings are bored out to supply oil to the bearings. Since the Citroen shaft has 3 mm less stroke than the original shaft, the rod of the 1200 cc VW Beetle, 3 mm longer, is used. Attempts to divide

the original shaft and equip it with other bearings failed. For the present standard mounting dimension, crankshafts with new measurements for the mounts have been made.

The problem of the Novotex wheels was solved with sets of gears made of plastic, or with thinner steel wheels that run just as quietly as the Novotex wheels did.

Getting away from the original condition, oilpans of aluminum instead of sheet steel are used. Even a set of all the springs can be supplied by the club on advance order. For electric power, there are thoroughly overhauled generators with new isolating technology. A French manufacturer is even planning to produce a 12-volt ignition-light set.

A restored Zündapp cycle usually requires countless hours of work, and it al-

most always looks as if it just rolled off the assembly line. It is all the more surprising when the odometer shows 40,000 or more kilometers. Most KS 600 and KS 601 models, including the original cutaway model, can be seen in the motorcycle collection of the Museum of Industry in Nuremberg.

The last machine owned by the company was driven on the stretches and to the control points of many off-road endurance trials until the seventies by Elisabeth Mann, the company founder's daughter, who donated it to the German Museum.

Even though more than forty years have passed since production was halted, many present-day KS 601 owners are not old grandfather types, but younger people. They know their "Green Elephants" to the last screw, and their shining eyes show how much they enjoy driving them.

Description of the KS 601 and KS 601 Sport Motorcycles

The Type KS 601 motorcycle of the Zündapp-Werke G.m.b.H. firm of Nuremberg and Munich was produced in series beginning with chassis no. 550 001, and Type KS 601 Sport beginning with chassis no. 54 001. The dimensions and values of the two types are identical. Derivatives of the KS 601 Sport are noted separately.

1. Chassis
a. Manufacturer and type	Zündapp-Werke GmbH, Nüremberg-Munich, Nüremberg works, KS 601
b. Power transmission	Chain and cone wheels
c. Chassis	Closed tube frame

2. Powerplant
a. Manufacturer and type	Zündapp-Werke GmbH, Nuremberg-Munich, Nuremberg works, KS 601
b. Type	Internal combustion engine, carburetor
c. Functioning	Four-stroke
d. KS 601 power	28 hp at 4700 rpm (15 minutes)
KS 601 Sport power	34 hp at 4700 rpm
Maximum power	38.5 hp at 6400 rpm
Dönsch values	35 hp at 6100 rpm
Maximum torque	4.9 mkg at 3550 rpm
e. Displacement	592 cc
f. Number of cylinders	Two
g. Bore	75 mm diameter
h. Stroke	67.6 mm
i. Cooling	Air cooling when in motion
k. Lubrication	Oil pump

3. Transmission
a. Manufacturer and type	Zündapp-Werke GmbH, Nuremberg-Munich, Nuremberg works, KS 601
b. Number of speeds	Four
c. Gear ratios	1st gear 1:3, 2nd gear 1:1.625, 3rd gear 1:1.238, 4th gear 1:0.962
d. Motor-to-gear ratio	1:1

e. Gear-to-axle ratio	Solo	Sidecar
	1:4.88	1:6.14
Total ratio, 1st gear	1:14.63	1:18.41
2nd gear	1:7.92	1:9.98
3rd gear	1:6.03	1:7.60
4th gear	1:4.69	1:5.90

4. Clutch
two-plate dry

5. Shifting
foot shifting

6. Tires
a. Front	3.50-19 on 2.15 B x 19 rim
b. Rear on sidecar	3.50-19 on 2.15 B x 19 rim, 4.00-19

7. Suspension
Telescopic front and rear wheel

8. Saddle
Pressure-spring saddle

9. Brake system
a. Brake type	Mechanical interior shoe
Hand brake	Cable-oparated, on front wheel
Foot brake	Mechanical, by rod, on rear wheel
b. Manufacturer	Zündapp-Werke GmbH Nuremberg-Munich, Nuremberg works

c. Dimensions	
Hand brake	230 mm drum diameter, 25 mm width, effective surface 2 x 48.5 sq.cm.
Foot brake	230 mm drum diameter, 25 mm width, effective surface 2 x 48.5 sq.cm.

d. Transition	to brake lever	to surface
Foot brake	1:29.9	1:59.8
Hand brake	1.48.9	1.97.8

10. Electrics
a. Ignition	-
b. Generator	Noris DS plate dynamo a 6/90 L
c. Lighting	Hella-Tacho headlight with Bilux lamp 35/35 W; 1.5 W parking light and lock-brake-rear license-plate light SBKR 62/1 with 3 W bulb and
d. Signal horn	100 x 6 DIN 72 701

11. Fuel tank
14.5 liter total (includes 2.5 liter reserve)

12. Muffler
Oval metal muffler divided internally into two chambers; exhaust flows through one chamber, then the other; a tube connects them

13. Top speed of KS 601 sitting upright with passenger	Solo	Sidecar
	123 kph	100 kph

KS 601 Sport	Solo	Sidecar
lying	153.2 kph	
sitting upright	143.4 kph	
with passenger	123 kph	110 kph

14. Dry weight of KS 601	225 kg	351 kg
KS 601 Sport	219 kg	345 kg

15. Load limit of KS 601	382 kg	583 kg
KS 601 Sport	376 kg	577 kg

16. Axle pressure of KS 601		Solo	Sidecar
a. No driver or passenger	front	103 kg	113 kg
	rear	122 kg	155 kg
	sidecar	83 kg	
b. With driver	front	128 kg	138 kg
	rear	172 kg	205 kg
	sidecar	83 kg	
c. Driver & passenger	front	130 kg	153 kg
	rear	252 kg	223 kg
	sidecar	125 kg	
d. With three persons	front	155 kg	
	rear	303 kg	
	sidecar	125 kg	
KS 601 Sport		Solo	Sidecar
a. No driver or passenger	front	100 kg	110 kg
	rear	119 kg	152 kg
	sidecar	83 kg	

KS 601

KS 601 Sport

b. With driver	front	125 kg	135 kg
	rear	169 kg	202 kg
	sidecar	83 kg	
c. Driver & passenger	front	127 kg	150 kg
	rear	249 kg	220 kg
	sidecar	125 kg	
d. With three persons	front	152 kg	
	rear	300 kg	
	sidecar	125 kg	

17. Steering
a. Type   Double-arm handlebars
b. Steering angle   ca. 64 degrees
c. Backswing   ca. 71 mm (with normal load)

18. Brake test with three persons
a. Hand brake   3.2 m.sec
b. Fiit brake   3.3 m/sec

19. Main dimensions of the KS 601
a. Wheelbase   ca. 1415 mm
b. Overall length   ca. 2140 mm
c. Overall width   ca. 765 mm, sidecar 865 mm
d. Overall height   ca. 1010 mm
e. Ground clearance   ca. 125 mm

    KS 601 Sport
a. Wheelbase   ca. 1415 mm
b. Overall length   ca. 2140 mm
c. Overall width   Solo ca. 680 mm at motor, sidecar ca. 765 mm
d. Overall height   ca. 1010 mm

20. Chassis and Motor Numbers
a. Chassis number   At right on steering head
b. Motor number   Under left cylinder on crankcase

In this form the motorcycle was first raced.

The last advertising photo of the **KS 601.**

Werner Kritter with a flat sidecar tire in an Alpine mountain test.

Additional hydraulic shock absorbers in the rear suspension of the racing machine.

The KS 601 first competed in the North Bavarian reliability run on 10/8/1950. At the start of the night stage are Weiss and Brendel with the new KS 601, behind them Hans Ernst on the old KS 600.

One of the few solo sporting events for the KS 601 was the eight-hour run at Solitude near Stuttgart. Here Georg Weiss is checked by longtime testmaster Hans Hofmann. At left in the Zündapp pit is Director Dr. Eitel-Friedrich Mann.

For the first time since World War II, German drivers were allowed to take part in the international six-day run—this time in Italy. Weiss and Brendel (76) and Keitel and Seemann (85), seen here in the final race at Monza, won gold medals and international acclaim.

XIIth ADAC Deutschlandfahrt, 1952: Technical service before the start at Bad Reichenhall. Number 22 is Hans Ernst with passenger Sörgel, 221 Gustav Keitel with Seemann.

Ernst and Sörgel on an off-road stage in the 1952 Deutschlandfahrt.

Gustav Keitel in the notorious "Wasserböden" mud course in the 1952 Sixdays at Bad Aussee, Austria.

The 1952 Sixdays results are featured in a newspaper advertisement.

DMV two-day run, 1953: Keitel and Müller, along with Weiss and Mages, and Ernst and Sörgel, were the only sidecar teams who finished penalty-free.

The final race of the 1953 DMV two-day run on the old Hockenheim-Ring was finished by the three Zündapp teams at an average speed of 117 kph.

Welcoming the victorious Zündapp team after the 1953 DMV two-day run: from right to left, Ernst and Sörgel, Weiss and Mages, and Keitel and Müller.

Austrian Alpenfahrt, 1953: Weiss and Mages won the coveted "Edelweiss" after scoring best time in the hill climb.

Nürnberg policemen Käser and Maurer took part in the bitter cold 1955 ADAC Wintersternfahrt, with Georg Weiss as team manager. Käser and Maurer were 1957 German off-road champions in the heavy sidecar class.

The last competitive appearance of the KS 601, with Kritter and Kreutzer, in the 1956 International Alpenfahrt.

Even drivers from lands behind the Iron Curtain had a Zündapp works entry in the 1956 Sixdays in Garmisch-Partenkirchen. Here, the Poles Baczkowski and Dziednig are fighting their way up the old Ettaler Berg course.

Racing at top speed for 24 hours at the notorious Bol d'Or in Montlhéry, France, where Werner Kritter (with ballast instead of a passenger) won his class in record time. Beside him is Richard Kessler on a Zündapp 250 solo cycle, the winner in his class.

Rudi Grenz and Heinz Kittler in the "North Bavarian."

For a planned world record attempt, this supercharged four-cylinder 1000 cc king shafts motor was built in 1938-39. What with the war, the record run never took place, but couldn't a production engine have looked like that later?

Thus ended the 1954 30,000 kilometer round-the-world trip by father and son Lange, seen arriving in Nürnberg.

The Langes' cycle was dismantled and examined by specialist journalists and factory technicians after their trip.